holiday (HOL - ~~...day~~). ~~...day~~ ...~~...~~
or the law dictates a halting of general business activity
to commemorate or celebrate a particular event. 2. A
religious feast day; a holy day. 3. A day free from work
that one may spend at leisure; a day off.
— American Heritage Dictionary

TABLE of CONTENTS

* These holidays are federally paid holidays for employees of the
  US government. Private companies and businesses may or may
  not recognize or count them as paid holidays.

Labor Day

Labor Day is a day that celebrates all the many kinds of working people and their various occupations. Its origin came about as a direct result of the Industrial Revolution in America and its volatile impact on society. It is celebrated in the US, Puerto Rico and Canada on the first Monday in September and unofficially marks the end of summer. In other countries Labor Day is similarly recognized on May 1st, but is known as May Day.

The Industrial Revolution began in England in the 1700's but didn't reach America until the 1800's. This movement began a series of sweeping changes in the vocational life of millions of people. Machines were invented and factories were developed to make all kinds of goods that were previously handmade. While factory work provided a new source of labor, it also became synonymous with long hours, dirty and sometimes dangerous working conditions. Because the mindset of the people generally was slower to catch up to the unique challenges and opportunities the Revolution generated, government legislative action to protect workers lagged behind the need. Thus unions, first called "combinations," were formed by workers grouping together who wanted some guarantees for job benefits, such as a fair wage and safe working conditions.

Along with 8 fellow workers, Uriah Stevens, a tailor in Philadelphia, PA, founded the Noble Order of Knights of Labor in 1869. This union first spread to other garment workers and later to other trades and industries. After the railway strikes in 1877 which led to arrests, mob violence, numerous deaths and $80 million of property damage primarily to industries and factories, the Knights of Labor grew to over 600,000 by 1886. This union was instrumental in supporting an idea conceived by two New York City tradesmen, Matthew Maguire, a machinist from Paterson, NJ, and Peter J. McGuire, a New York City carpenter who also the United Brotherhood of Carpenters and Joiners, another union. These two men organized the first Labor Day parade in New York City in September in 1882. Other unions caught on and began to push state governments for similar activities. Five years later, Oregon became the first state to declare Labor Day an official holiday. A few other states slowly began to follow Oregon's lead.

It was not until 1894 that Labor Day became a national holiday. The Pullman railway strike caused numerous upheavals in Chicago and Cleveland. US mail service had been interrupted. A federal court then ordered the strikers to return to work. When they refused, President Grover Cleveland ordered federal troops to break the strike. The troops were successful. While most Americans approved of Cleveland's action, the unions were naturally upset. To help mend the differences he had with unions and workers, Cleveland in 1894 signed into law Labor Day as a national holiday that would be celebrated on the first Monday in September.

Some unions and other labor organizations sponsor Labor Day activities, although there are no real national customs related to the holiday. Most Americans enjoy it simply as a day off from work and spend the day as they please. While many people in the States may complain about their jobs, most are probably grateful for gainful employment, job benefits and the comparative stability and prosperity they enjoy.

For Christians, the Bible teaches that our talents and skills, as well as the opportunity to work, are all gifts from God. Work is to be pursued with joy and commitment, and Christians are to serve their employer as they would if it were done unto God Himself (Ephesians 6:5-8). In contrast to one day a year in recognition of work, the Bible says that the seven day work week is to have one day of rest (Genesis 2:2), typically called a Sabbath (rest) day. Most Christians set aside Sunday as their day of rest. The focus on Sunday is for worshiping God, recognizing and thanking Him for all that He has done for His people and the world.

Columbus Day

Columbus Day is the day named for the famed explorer, Christopher Columbus, Admiral of the Ocean Sea. The holiday falls on October 12th, the date he discovered land in what was called the "New World." In the US the holiday is celebrated on the second Monday in October, although many South American countries still celebrate it on October 12th.

Columbus has been increasingly maligned in modern times for many reasons, and studying him reveals many enigmas in his character. Some recent historians say that Columbus' arrival was the worst thing that ever happened to natives of North America, since it began the period of European exploration and colonialization. History does show that much harm came as a result of Columbus' adventuresome spirit. But the actions of others can hardly be blamed on him. This more modern viewpoint also presupposes that natives living in the Western Hemisphere posed little or no danger to themselves or each other. Such is hardly the case, as numerous tribes had territorial ambitions, fought constantly, and in some cases offered human sacrifices and even practiced cannibalism! We can only guess what life would have been like for American natives as well as for Europeans and the rest of the world had Columbus not made his important discovery. The fact of the matter is, he did, and what follows is a summary of the events of his life.

"Columbus" is the English name for Colombo, his family's Italian name. Christopher was the first of five children born in Genoa to his father, Domenico Colombo. His mother was Susanna Fontanarossa, a daughter of a wool weaver. His younger brothers, Bartholomew and Diego, worked closely with him in his enterprises. Christopher helped his father make fabric on the loom, but he longed to go to sea. Although he had little formal education, he learned to speak Spanish and taught himself Latin, the language of geography at the time. He ventured into sailing as short term opportunities arose. On one such venture he sailed to England with part of a convoy. The convoy was attacked by raiders off the coast of Lagos, Portugal. Wounded in the melee, Columbus jumped from the sinking ship, grabbed a long oar which kept him afloat and made it safely to the coast.

In the second half of the 1400's thinking people had already realized that the earth was round. While some of Columbus' motivation was to find a trade route to the Indies (Indonesia, Japan, China, etc.), there was something else driving him. In his personal journal he wrote:

It was the Lord who put into my mind (I could feel his hand upon me) the fact that it would be possible to sail from here to the Indies. All who heard of my project rejected it with laughter, ridiculing me. There is no question that the inspiration was from the Holy Spirit, because He comforted me with rays of marvelous inspiration from the Holy Scriptures.

One such section of Scripture that Columbus quoted was from the Old Testament book of Isaiah, chapter 49, which says,

Listen to me, you islands, and hear this, you distant nations: Before I was born the Lord called me; from my birth he has made mention of my name...I will also make you a light for the Gentiles [nations], that you may bring my salvation to the ends of the earth" (verses 1,6).

Columbus understood these verses to apply personally of him. He even pointed to his own name "Christopher," which means *Christ-bearer*, as proof of his divine appointment to sail to the "ends of the earth" with God's message of salvation. As of this writing Columbus' journal has not been translated into English.

Columbus' venture of sailing west to find the East was rejected by the kings of Portugal and England, due in part to his vast underestimation of the size of the ocean. However, after some delay King Ferdinand and Queen Isabella of Spain decided to support the ambitious man from Genoa. He sailed from Palos, Spain on August 3, 1492 in three ships that held a total of 90 men. The famous ships — the *Pinta, Nina,* and *Santa*

Maria —were *caravels*, newly designed vessels that would navigate headwinds more efficiently. During the trip Columbus wrote in his diary, "For the execution of the journey to the Indies, I did not make use of intelligence, mathematics or maps. It is simply the fulfillment of what Isaiah had prophesied..." He truly sensed God was guiding him.

The threat of mutiny on October 10th almost ruined the voyage and history. After sailing west for over 3 weeks without seeing any land, the sailors had had enough and demanded to turn around. Columbus requested only 3 more days of sailing; if no land was spotted by then, then turn around they would! Land was sighted on October 12th at 2:00 AM. Hours later Columbus, followed by others, marched ashore on an island of the Bahamas he named San Salvador (meaning *Holy Savior*), knelt and kissed the beach, planted a cross "as a token of Jesus Christ our Lord and in honor of the Christian faith" and prayed,

> *"O Lord, Almighty and everlasting God, by Thy Holy Word Thou hast created the heaven and the earth, and the sea; blessed and glorified be Thy name, and praised be Thy Majesty, which hath deigned to use us, Thy humble servants, that Thy holy Name may be proclaimed in this second part of the earth."*

In spite of his efforts to please God, all did not go well. A lack of gold discoveries gave rise to frequent dissension among the sailors. Thinking he had landed in the Indies, he forcibly took some "Indians," now known as Native Americans, back to Spain with him. His second and third trips, although much larger expeditions which led to more discoveries, also proved frustrating and included their own shares of struggles and disappointments. Native unrest, colony rebellion, loss of ships and lives, loss of popular support back home and imprisonment were some of the ordeals he faced.

His fourth and final voyage in 1502 was his most enjoyable. He took along his 13 year old son, Ferdinand, and numerous other older boys who were better company than the "old salts" (older seamen) who constantly complained. In present day Panama he was told of another great (Pacific) ocean, but he never saw it. This last trip took him two and one half years, since he was marooned for one year in

Jamaica. By the time he returned, Queen Isabella had died and King Ferdinand would have nothing more to do with him. By this time he was 53, and his health was failing. Having enough money on which to live, his "retirement" was brief. He died on May 20, 1506 in the presence of his two sons and numerous faithful servants and a few close friends.

The trade route to the Indies was not clearly established until Magellan's voyage circumnavigated the world 16 years after Columbus' death. When Columbus set foot in South America (Venezuela), he wrote in his journal, "I believe that this is a very great continent which until today has been unknown." He thought then and died thinking that this continent was somewhere south of China. He never knew he discovered a whole new region of the world previously unexplored by Europeans.

The New World is named for Italian explorer Amerigo Vespucci, who claimed its discovery on a voyage in 1497. Columbus never disputed the claim because he thought the islands he explored were part of the Indies. He first set foot on the South American mainland a year after Vespucci's claim. In 1507 someone suggested that this new continent be called America "because Amerigo discovered it." Although scholars have long since rejected Vespucci's claim of discovery, the name caught on, and the two American continents, North and South, had their names. But the Republic of Columbia bears the Admiral's name, as do countless rivers, cities, streets, buildings, aircraft, boats, etc.

Columbus Day was first celebrated in New York City in 1792 when people celebrated the 300th anniversary of his discovery. President Benjamin Harrison called upon the people to set aside the day 100 years later at the 400th anniversary. Although generally very festive in 1992, the 500th anniversary was a worldwide event that revealed some questioning of Columbus' rightful place in history. The holiday has been celebrated annually in the US since 1920. There are virtually no customs associated with this holiday, but may include parades, speeches, outdoor activities named for the explorer (for example, the "Columbus Day Regatta"). The holiday is much more eventful in South America.

Halloween

The modern celebrations of Halloween in America come from ancient pagan religious practices, many of which have lost their original meaning. *Pagan* means any religion that is not associated with traditional, Biblical Christianity. Halloween has also been strongly associated with the *Occult*, which means "hidden," "covered up," or "secret." Occult stands for hidden evil, and finds its source ultimately in an evil, spiritual being Christians call *the Devil* or *Satan*. These names are found in the Bible. The Bible strongly opposes the nature of Halloween festivities. While many modern day practices of Halloween are superficial, real acts of evil, including harmful and criminal activities associated with the holiday, are increasing. Safety for children has become a major concern for parents. Thus the level of Christianity's effect on American culture may impact the seriousness of Halloween celebrations and how much Halloween's religious practices return to their original intentions.

American Halloween practices have three primary sources that have merged together. These three sources follow with some detailed elaborations.

Pre-Christian England, Scotland & Ireland

Before the arrival of Christianity in England, the religion of the Celtic peoples, there was Druidism, a pantheistic religion of spirit beings in nature. The priestly class was known as the Druids. One of their chief deities was Saman. The Druids believed that Saman would call forth the spirits of the dead on October 31st, the last day of the Celtic calendar. (October is the month signalling the coming of winter and the "season of dying" — when leaves fall from trees and animals prepare for hibernation.) This day, new year's eve, was called *Samhain* (pronounced Sah WEEN). They believed that on the last day of the year the normal borders between the natural and spiritual worlds in the universe were temporarily suspended. Thus these spirits, many of which were evil, had free access to human activity on earth. Consequently, animal (and sometimes human) sacrifices were made. Internal organs were spilled out to determine the future for people, and to appease any evil spirit that might be around. Bodies of sacrificed animals were piled up and burned in "bonefires," later called *bonfires.* These fires also were said to drive away evil spirits who supposedly did not like all the light given off by the flames.

Other practices developed. If no spirits caused mischief to a family, a celebration would occur later that night. To celebrate, families would collect food from neighbors and friends. Children went from house to house collecting the needed items. Often their parents would dress them up as a ghost, goblin (a grave-robbing creature) or ghoul (an ugly ghost) so that if the children ran into an evil spirit, the spirit would think the children were one of them and do them no harm! Later the children began to act out what they heard the spirits were doing. Thus came the greeting, *Trick or Treat!* Either the families would be generous and add to the kids' collection (give a treat), or they would act like an evil spirit and play a "trick", such as dumping over garbage cans, taking off fence gates, painting graffiti on a house or barn, letting pets or farm animals loose, etc. Turnips were carved out with ugly or scary faces to chase off or scare away any evil spirits contemplating a visit. People put apples in a large bucket of water and tried to "bob" for them, picking them out using only their teeth. They believed that if they were successful (apples representing favor or blessing), no evil spirit would bother them that night.

Witches of Central Europe
When Christianity arrived in Central Europe the people already had a strong belief in witchcraft, also known as Black Magic. Witchcraft is the religion of evil, where a witch (female) and warlock (male) had direct or close contact with the Devil, the ultimate source of evil in the world. These individuals were greatly feared. Black was their chosen representative color. Creatures such as cats and bats were thought to be witches or warlocks having the ability to change into those animal forms and back again. (Spiders were later added.) Witches were thought to have the ability to fly on broomsticks.

Witches have several "high holy days" or "Witches Sabbaths" (religious days) throughout the year. One of them is the first day in May (May Day). The last such special day in the year for witches (similar to the Druids) is October 31st. Typically this was a night of feasting, partying and revelry. They used carved out pumpkins to represent evil spirits with which they were in contact. Witches believed that all spells they had cast throughout the year, if they had not yet been effective, would all take effect on the night of October 31st. Thus for them it was a night of glorying in the power of the devil.

The Roman Catholic Church

Strange as it may seem, the Roman Catholic Church (RCC) also added to the Halloween tradition, although the exact opposite was probably the church leaders' intention! Christendom is generally divided between Catholic and Protestant groups. There are some clear differences between Catholic and non-Catholic Christian teaching. While the RCC does teach from the Bible, it also includes church tradition as a source of authority for practice. One church practice, praying to or with dead saints, has an apparent similarity to Halloween's preoccupation with the dead.

As many Christians were martyred for their faith in the early centuries of Christianity, some Christians wanted to remember them as a special kind of people. So organizers of formal, organized Christianity (later, the RCC) classified them as "saints." Later the martyrdom requirement was dropped, and more and more people became "saints" after their death. After some time the number of saints greatly multiplied, and there were not enough days in the year to honor them all. Thus the idea of an "All Saints Day" developed. Although it was originally celebrated in the Spring, RCC Pope Gregory III in 732 AD changed it to November 1st. It was called *Allhallowmas*, meaning "all saints mass" (*mass* meaning RCC worship ceremony). The church also decided that the evening before, October 31st, could begin the *Allhallowmas,* so church members began attending churches to pray to the dead, while those not connected to the church were likewise preoccupied with dead spirits. The name for this October 31st service developed when the "All" dropping off from *Allhallowmas*, and the "mas" was changed to "evening' or "e'en." What was left was "Hallowe'en" or *Halloween.* RCC members believed that the saints to which they prayed were intercessors for them to God, and could bless them. There was a saint for travel, a saint for financial success, a saint for healing, one for children, etc. etc. The idea that the dead can bless someone in this way developed from RCC tradition and is not found in the Bible. Therefore this attempt resulted in causing great confusion among church members at that time of the year.

The answer to the question, *Why did Pope Gregory III change Allhallowmas to November 1st?* is not clear. Most probably he thought that since the people were already in a celebrating mood, the church might try to "Christianize" the pagan holiday. Experts consider the attempt a complete failure. The exact opposite occurred! Today, many many Catholics (as well as Protestants) get involved in various Halloween activities with apparently little or no understanding of their original intent or meaning.

Martin Luther

Another important event happened on October 31st. Martin Luther, a RCC priest who was studying the Bible, became increasingly dissatisfied with the teachings of the RCC. In 1517 AD he posted 95 complaints or statements (called *theses)* on the door of the Wittenberg Church in Germany. Soon afterwards he left the RCC and began what is now called the *Reformation,* which created the Protestant branch of Christendom. Catholics originally saw Protestants as heretics (deniers of the faith), while Protestants saw themselves as returning to the true teachings of the Bible. What Martin Luther did was draw attention, not to RCC teaching, but to God's Word. In this connection, the Bible says that all forms of witchcraft, necromancy (preoccupation with dead things), seances (meetings with the spirits of the dead), demon activity, human sacrifice, all occultism, superstitious practices, fortune telling, astrology, etc. are to be rejected and avoided (Deuteronomy 18:10-12). All such things are evil. At this writing, not all of God's people are being obedient. However, it appears that more and more Christians in America are following this command. Some do not celebrate Halloween at all, while others have replaced Halloween with alternative activities, a few being harvest festivals and/or costume parties with Christian themes.

Veterans Day

Veterans Day is a patriotic day set aside for everyone who served in the United States Armed Forces. It is celebrated on the fourth Monday in October. The following is a brief history of how this holiday developed.

In 1919 after the end of World War I, President Woodrow Wilson declared November 11th as "Armistice Day" which commemorated the end of that war. Originally it was to be a day of mourning for those who died in that war. Then in 1938 Congress passed a law which made Armistice Day a federal holiday. This change came on the heels of a growing movement of veterans related issues that began with WWI veterans. The Veterans Administration, a Cabinet Level department of the government, had been approved earlier in 1930. At that time Armistice Day was still celebrated on November 11th.

With the passing of World War II and the Korean War, people realized that to be fair to veterans of these and later wars, Armistice Day would either need to be changed or other holidays would need to be adopted. Thus Congress chose the most simple solution and in 1954 changed the name to Veterans Day. This step broadened the scope of the day to include not only war veterans, but all veterans, whether or not they served their country in wartime. More recently Veterans Day was designated as the fourth Monday of October.

Celebrations for this holiday include parades, speeches, tributes, displays of the American flag and other related activities. In Washington, DC, a special ceremony is held at the Tomb of the Unknown Soldier. Many Americans will simply spend the day doing something pleasurable, relaxing, fun or use it in some other discretionary manner.

Christians as a whole don't make any particular religious associations with this holiday, although some connections could be made in terms of serving others, entering into spiritual battles, etc. Generally they celebrate it as other citizens of the US do.

Thanksgiving

Thanksgiving is a holiday specifically set aside for the purpose of thanking God for His provisions and blessings. It may be the oldest, continually-celebrated holiday in America and has a very rich tradition behind it. Many countries of the world don't have a similar day set aside for expressing thankfulness to God. Although this holiday began as a religiously-oriented event, this aspect has diminished in modern times. A thorough survey of the background and history of Thanksgiving follows. Unfortunately most of this information is *not* taught today to American students in public schools.

The Pilgrims

England in the 1500's was a monarchy. In 1534 the Act of Supremacy made the king the leader of the Church of England. Everyone there was considered a member of this church, whether or not the religious decrees of the king were based on Biblical truth. A number of his religious decrees were not well received by segments of the population. Thus developed groups of people who disagreed with the king's religious orders. Today they might be called "religious dissidents." However, Bible believing Christians wanted to be loyal to God and true to the Bible. They called themselves *pilgrims*, meaning a foreigner, alien or wanderer, one who sees this life as preparation for the next life. This idea comes from the Bible (Hebrews 11:9,13-16).

The Pilgrims were not united as to how they would respond to the king's religious orders. Some of them wanted to remain in the Church of England to reform and "purify" it. This group became known as the "Puritans." Others wanted to leave the Church completely, so some called them "Separatists." This latter group continued to call themselves "Pilgrims," and that is what they are known as today. Both contained dedicated believers in God and the Bible; they simply differed as to how they would deal with a king who had become very hostile towards them. There were many more Puritans than Pilgrims, the latter numbering fewer than a thousand.

Pilgrims stopped attending worship services in churches and held services in their homes. The king was completely intolerant of such activities and had them hunted down like criminals, jailed and persecuted. In 1607 they began leaving England for Leyden (pronounced LIE den), Holland. Then in 1618 King James I decreed that all remaining Pilgrims in England must either conform to the Church or leave the country. Those that had not yet left did so rapidly.

Leyden, Holland
In Leyden the Pilgrims, although model citizens, were penniless internationals who qualified for only the lowest paying jobs. Although *they had the freedom to worship as they chose*, they wanted to preserve their worship practices in their native language — English. Their children were beginning to speak Dutch, and this, combined with their economic difficulties, convinced them that God wanted them to sail to America and begin all over again. Below are some of their leaders

John Carver — one of the "chief men," First Governor of the new settlement.
William Bradford — one of the "chief men," English farmer, Second Governor.
John Robinson — Pastor of the Pilgrims.
William Brewster — Elder of the church, temporary pastor.
Captain Miles Standish — Dutch military veteran (not a Christian).
Dr. Samuel Fuller — medical doctor.
Edward Winslow — another of the "chief men," first white man to meet the Indian chief, Massasoit, first man to marry in North America.

Sailing Across the Atlantic
Two ships were originally prepared to take them to America: *The Speedwell*, and the better known *Mayflower*. The Pilgrims left Leyden on a barge to Delftshaven, boarded the *Speedwell* and set sail on July 22, 1620 for Southampton to join those on the *Mayflower*. Aboard the *Mayflower* were about 80 "strangers." Some of these later additions were sympathetic to the Pilgrims' struggles; others were going to pursue dreams of material prosperity. Both ships set sail August 5th, but early, recurring problems with the *Speedwell* forced them to return to Plymouth. They sold the *Speedwell* and squeezed as many passengers and as much cargo into the *Mayflower* as possible. In all, 102 men, women and children set sail again.

Nearly halfway across the Atlantic, an extremely violent storm (probably a hurricane) broke the cross-beam of the ship which supported the main mast. They were able to temporarily repair it. On November 9th, "Land, ho!" rang out. They quickly learned that the storm had blown them to Cape Cod, over 100 miles north of Virginia, their planned destination. If they settled in Cape Cod, they would be free from obligations to the New England Company, which had business dealings in Virginia at the Jamestown colony. They decided the storm had been providential, that God wanted them to be in Cape Cod. So they settled there, and formed a new kind of government, based upon the *Mayflower Compact*. It follows:

In the name of God, amen. We whose names are underwritten, the loyal subjects of our dread Sovereign Lord, King James by the Grace of God, of Great Britain, France, Ireland, King, Defender of the Faith, etc. Having undertaken, for the glory of God, and advancement of the Christian Faith, and honor of our King and country, a voyage to plant the first colony in the northern parts of Virginia, do by these presents solemnly and mutually in the presence of God and one of another, covenant and combine ourselves together into a civil body politic, for our better ordering and preservation and furtherance of the ends aforesaid, and by virtue hereof to enact, constitute and frame such just and equal laws, ordinances, acts, constitutions and offices from time to time, as shall be thought most meet and convenient for the general good of the colony, unto which we promise all due submission and obedience. In witness whereof we have hereunder subscribed our names at Cape Cod, the 11th of November, in the year of the reign of our Sovereign King James of England. . .Anno Domini 1620.

Notice that this document clearly shows that at least one of the Pilgrims' purposes was "the advancement of the Christian faith." It is also true that this document was the beginnings of self-government in the modern world. It was made possible because of the Christian virtue of self-control.

Plymouth

The Pilgrims found an area already cleared to farm. Nearby were four spring-fed creeks. They named their community *Plymouth* because they last received help from other Christians in Plymouth in England. The *Mayflower* stayed to house them until cabins were built. On January 14th, a roof fire on the Common House nearly killed them all because of the gun powder inside. But from December, 1620 through March, 1621 forty-seven died of disease and infection, including 13 of the 18 wives. While 45% of them died, they were still grateful. The death toll at Jamestown had been nearly twice as high!

Samoset and Squanto

In mid-March, 1621 an Indian marched into the Common House where the Pilgrims were being instructed about military defense. "Welcome," he said in perfect English, and then asked for something to eat. They gave him only English foods (biscuit and butter with cheese, roast duck, pudding and brandy), and he enjoyed it all. After eating, he revealed his name: *Samoset.* He was from a tribe in Maine and loved to travel. He learned English from traveling with sea captains. He told them that the land on which the Pilgrims settled had belonged to the Patuxet Indians, a violent and barbarous tribe that died from a mysterious plague four years earlier. After spending the night with them, Samoset returned one week later with another Indian who spoke fluent English: *Squanto.* He was a *Patuxet!* In 1605 Squanto and four others of his tribe were captured and taken back to England. There they learned English and were separated. Squanto returned to his homeland 9 years later with Captain John Smith (of Jamestown). Almost immediately another captain seized him again, took him and other Indians to Malaga, Spain, and sold them as slaves. Some friars (monks) purchased him and introduced him to the Christian faith. They later released him, and Squanto made his way back to England. He finally persuaded Captain Dermer to take him back to America in 1619, one year before the Pilgrims left Plymouth. Six months before the Pilgrims landed, he found that his entire tribe had died. He found refuge in another tribe to the southwest headed by Chief Massasoit.

Peace Treaty

With Samoset as interpreter, Massasoit came to meet the Englishmen. Edward Winslow was the Pilgrim representative. With some fanfare, gift-giving and speeches, Massasoit made a forty-year peace treaty with the newcomers guaranteeing mutual assistance and aid. Interestingly enough, Massasoit was probably the only other Indian chief (besides Powhatan near Jamestown) who would accept the foreigners as friends.

Spring and Summer, 1621

Good and bad things happened during this time. The *Mayflower* finally left for England April 21st. Governor Carver died (probably of a cerebral hemorrhage) and was replaced by William Bradford. But the building and planting continued. Squanto showed them how to plant, fish, hunt and make clothing. Edward Winslow, who had lost his wife in the "General Sickness," married Susanna White, who had similarly lost her husband. While life was difficult and strenuous, these first Christian people in North America were full of thanksgiving to God for his mercies.

A Declaration, A Feast

Governor Bradford proclaimed a day of public thanksgiving to God to be held in October. Massasoit was invited and showed up a day early with 90 Indians! Fortunately they brought with them 5 dressed deer, more than 12 fat, wild turkeys, and eight different types of vegetables. The Indian women taught the Pilgrim wives how to make cornmeal pudding, fruit pies, maple syrup, and another Indian treat — *popcorn!* Between the meals, athletic games and contests of various skills were held. The celebration went so well, it was extended for another 3 days!

Proclamations

Although the Thanksgiving celebration spread throughout the regions of the United States, it wasn't until America's first president, George Washington, declared the following statement in 1789:

Whereas it is the duty of all nations to acknowledge the providence of Almighty God, to obey His will, to be grateful for His benefits, and humbly to implore His protection and favor. . .I do recommend and assign Thursday, the 26th day of November next to be devoted by the people of these States to the service of that great and glorious Being, Who is the beneficent Author of all the good that was, that is, or that will be; that we may then all unite in rendering unto Him our sincere and humble thanks for His kind care and protection of the people of this country. . .

Later President Abraham Lincoln in 1863 set apart the last Thursday in November as the national holiday. It was at this time that family became an additional focus of the holiday. Finally in 1941, during Franklin D. Roosevelt's administration, Thanksgiving was declared to be on the fourth Thursday of November.

Celebrations

Much of the food served at modern Thanksgiving dinners includes most of the items from the very first celebration: turkey, ham, dressing, potatoes with gravy, numerous other vegetables, bread, and puddings and pies for dessert. Initially this meal was held to thank God for the blessings of a good crop, of having food for the winter. One table decoration many families use is the "horn of plenty," called a *cornucopia*, which means "abundance." Originally this was a curved goat's horn overflowing with fruit and grain. The meaning of this item explains why it was borrowed from Greek mythology where it represented an abundance of provisions. Modern cornucopias keep the same shape but are frequently made of straw like a basket.

Parades also accompany the Thanksgiving celebration. They began in the late 1800's. Modern "Turkey day" parades include a host of figures, floats, balloons and bands that may or may not necessarily have Thanksgiving themes connected with them. Many floats and balloon figures depict popular cartoon characters or represent corporate sponsors. Appearing on the last float at the end of most Thanksgiving parades is Santa Claus, the secular symbol of Christmas and gifts. His presence is the official sign that the Christmas holiday shopping season has begun.

Sometimes Americans have special church services where blessings are recounted and thanks is publicly given, especially, it seems, for family and friends. Thanksgiving is a very family oriented holiday. Relatives will often travel great distances to be with each other to celebrate. In fact, statistics show that Thanksgiving weekend is the busiest travel time of the entire year! With the advent of television, football seems to have become a fixture of modern American Thanksgiving. Although sporting events were held at the first Thanksgiving, the similarity between that and the preoccupation of football today is coincidental. Thanksgiving remains a unique holiday where people express their gratefulness for God and his blessings, primarily family and friends.

Christmas

Christmas is the holiday celebrating the birth of Jesus Christ. Although it is a religious holiday, many modern customs and practices associated with it were carried over from other festivals - some religious, some not. What follows is a little background, history and development of the American Christmas celebration.

The background and birth of Jesus can be found in the Bible, in the New Testament books of Matthew (chapters 1-2) and Luke (chapter 2). These two books, along with Mark and John, are called *Gospels*, meaning "good news." The birth of Jesus in Bethlehem signaled the fulfillment of a long awaited promise that God would send someone, his personal representative, to remove the negative effects of personal evil in the world. Jesus was that representative. Thus his arrival on the human scene, announced by a night sky full of angels (Luke 2:9-14), was good news. Shepherds were the first visitors to see the newborn Baby. Later wisemen, or *Magi*, traveled "from the east," to worship the Child and offer him gifts (Matthew 2:1-12). Early Christians did not initially celebrate this event because they considered celebrating birthdays to be a pagan (non-Christian) custom. However, the holiday gradually developed, beginning around 200 AD, and its celebration customs varied from country to country. Below is a brief summary of current American Christmas practices.

Date

The date of Christ's birth cannot be accurately determined. The December 25th date came about as a result of an attempt to "Christianize" a pagan holiday known as *Saturnalia*, which began December 17th and was noted for its unrestrained revelry and orgies. In 274 AD Roman Emperor Aurelian declared December 25th a holiday of the Syrian sun god, *Sol Invictus* ("Invincible Sun") throughout the empire. December 25th is the time of the winter solstice, where the sun is at the greatest distance from the equator. So the 25th marks the beginning of longer daylight. In 336 AD the Roman Emperor Constantine declared this day to be the celebration of Christ's birth, obviously trying to reorient the holiday for Christians. When the Empire split between east and west, the church in the east (Eastern Orthodox) recognized January 6th as the celebration date. In many countries January 6th is still honored as the "official" birth date of Christ. The time between December 25th and January 6th forms what has become known as the "12 Days of Christmas."

Names

"Christmas" comes from the early English phrase, *Christes Masse*, meaning "Christ's mass," the name of the Roman Catholic worship service held on December 25th. Another name for this season used by other churches and Christians is *Advent*, meaning "coming" or "arrival," an obvious reference to the long-awaited and much-anticipated birth of the Jewish Messiah, also called *Christ*. These terms mean "anointed or chosen one." The name *Yule* came from Scandinavia, and was originally a large log that was the foundation of the fire in the hearth in honor of their national god, Thor. When they converted to Christianity, "Yuletime" became synonymous with Christmas. Another word, *noel,* means "carol," a topic to be covered later. The abbreviation "Xmas" comes from the Greek letter, *chi (X)*, which begins Christ's name in Greek.

Saint Nicholas / Santa Claus

Saint Nicholas was a real historical figure of the 4th Century. He lived in ancient Asia Minor (modern-day Turkey), and was the Bishop of Myra. He was a devout and wealthy Christian pastor whose generosity became world famous. He used his wealth to help sailors, the poor, social outcasts, and children, especially orphans. On Christmas he would anonymously deliver gifts to orphanages for children. The Greek and Russian churches made him the patron saint of gifts, seafarers, scholars, virgins and children. The modern American Santa Claus bears virtually no resemblance to Saint Nicholas. Early Dutch settlers in New York called Saint Nicholas *Sinterklaas*, thus Santa Claus. Over the years the American Santa developed many of the secular characteristics of the British Santa, "Father Christmas," including entering a house through the chimney and stuffing stockings hung near the chimney. This idea came from an old Norse (Scandinavian) legend. But the American Santa became better defined in the 1800's. Clement Moore in 1822 first described Santa in a fur-trimmed suit leading a sleigh pulled by reindeer in his poem, "'Twas the Night Before Christmas." Later that century, cartoonist Thomas Nast produced a series of sketches that showed Santa as a jolly, plump winter-time visitor. Leaving toys and goodies for children seems to be about the only similarity between the ancient and modern figures. Christians and non-Christians today consider the modern American Santa Claus to be a secular representation of Christmas that has nothing to do with the historical events originating the holiday.

Christmas Tree / House Decorations

The origin of the Christmas tree is another tradition that cannot be accurately found. One story traces it to a Christian missionary named Boniface who lived in the 8th Century. He worked among the Germans and challenged the followers of the Druid religion in England. A later legend is that Martin Luther, leader of the Protestant Reformation in the 1500's, began the custom of decorating fir trees. Either way, the custom spread throughout countries where Christians were dominant. Ornaments on the trees vary from country to country. Decorating the home with plants also became popular. Scandinavians considered mistletoe to be a plant of peace and good will. Hanging evergreen branches (and later, wreaths) began with the Romans around New Year's and symbolized good luck. It is easy to see how these customs merged, due to the holidays being so close together. Holly later became a favorite decoration. Poinsettias, a green plant with red blooms native to Mexico, have been added to plant decorations in homes.

Christmas Cards / Gift Giving

Giving Christmas cards is a rather recent addition to the holiday. Handwritten notes of holiday greetings and wishes preceded card giving. It was an artist, John Calcott Horsley, who designed the first Christmas card in 1843. By the late 1860's, Christmas cards had become as popular as the handwritten messages. Around 1875 the first multicolored cards appeared. The giving of gifts has two possible origins. First, Christians point to the gifts of gold, frankincense and myrrh the wisemen gave to Baby Jesus. Secondly, Saint Nicholas's tradition of gift-giving is also cited. Either one reflects the kindness that God showed in giving His Son as a gift to the world. Both Christians and non-Christians enjoy this opportunity to express love by gift-giving.

Christmas Carols

The first Christmas hymns were written in the 5th Century. Originally composed in Latin, they contained primarily theological topics. Carols (*noels*), songs with more human and personal subjects, appeared in the 1200's. During the Middle Ages (900-1400 AD) people incorporated drama and plays into the celebration of Christmas. Carols became an integral part of these re-enactments. After the plays, carolers strolled down the street singing — thus, the birth of street caroling. Many of the traditional favorite Christmas carols, such as "O Come, All Ye Faithful" and "Silent Night," were written in the 1800's. Christmas songs such as "Jingle Bells" and "White Christmas" came later and reflect a more secular viewpoint of the holiday. Handel's *Messiah*, an oratorio (music drama without staging) first performed in 1742, is also a Christmas favorite. Musicologists agree that Christmas music is among the finest ever written in the world.

Star / Lights

Although some might point to *Saturnalia*, the holiday celebrating longer daylight, the Star of Bethlehem (Matthew 2:1-2) is the source for the presence of lights and stars as ornaments in Christmas decorations. These stars, usually strategically placed (such as at the top of Christmas trees or on rooftops), convey the idea of Jesus' birth in Bethlehem. The presence of lights inside and outside of houses convey the claim of Jesus when He said, *I am the light of the world* (John 8:12). The Bible pictures the world in spiritual darkness until the birth of Christ, and compares His birth to light penetrating a dark place (Luke 2:30-32 and John 1:4-5,9).

Foods

Although the foods served for Christmas dinner may vary from family to family (and from country to country), typical items usually found at an American family's Christmas dinner would include turkey and dressing (or sometimes chicken, duck, goose or ham), potatoes and gravy, sweet potatoes, green vegetables, cranberry sauce, nuts, fruits, fruit cake, plum pudding, pumpkin and/or mincemeat pies and sweets. Eggnog is usually the favorite drink for the whole family.

Nativity Scenes

Many American Christians set up a small nativity (sometimes called *creche*) scene in their homes, often under their Christmas trees, or a larger one outside in their yard. This contains figures of Baby Jesus in his first bed, which was called a "manger" (feeding trough). With him in the scene are his mother, Mary, and her husband Joseph. Also frequently included are the shepherds, wisemen and a few surrounding angels as well as some livestock animals, all thought to be present at that time. While the Christmas season has become very commercialized, the nativity scene represents the birth of Christ and draws us back to the real focus of the holiday — the humble and simple surroundings of Jesus, His life and message of God's forgiveness. He made this possible through His death and becomes available to all through simple faith in Him. His coming to earth is among the most significant events of history. Even our calendar dating system is based on the fact of His being here! Christmas honors the birth and coming of this most remarkable Person.

Candy Canes

The red and white striped candy cane has become one of the most popular symbols of Christmas. It was designed by a candy maker in Indiana. He thought about several aspects of Christmas and incorporated these ideas into the candy cane's design. The pure white represents both the virgin birth of Jesus and His sinless life on earth. On many canes there are large and smaller stripes. The smaller red stripes symbolize the "stripes" Jesus received when He was whipped shortly before He died. The larger red stripe stands for his blood which was shed as he died on the cross. The candy maker made the cane from a hard candy formula, the hardness representing Jesus as "the Rock" (see 1 Corinthians 10:4). The curled top makes it appear as a shepherd's staff, another reference to Jesus when he said, "I am the Good Shepherd" (John 10:11). Upside down, the cane forms the letter 'J,' the first name of Jesus! Most of these symbols are not commonly known today.

Celebrations

The specifics of family Christmas celebrations can have as many variations as there are families. Typically families will open presents either on Christmas Eve or Christmas Day. Members may open them at the same time, one at a time, or have some other type of family tradition. Many Christian families will have a birthday cake for Jesus, and sing "Happy Birthday" to Him, in keeping with American birthday celebrations. Some may sing Christmas carols together, share meaningful Christmas stories, or enter in on a family project designed to help others less fortunate than they. Many churches will have special meetings (such as Christmas Eve services) or regular services with Christmas themes. Many churches help the community celebrate with special events such as Christmas pageants, plays or dramas, concerts or "singing Christmas trees." Or they may help the community with a particular assistance program, such as feeding the poor and homeless, sending gifts to prisoners and their families, sending packages to military personnel separated from family during the holidays, or a wide variety of other such beneficial projects. All such activities come this time of year primarily because God gave His best, His son Jesus, to the world. Christmas is a season where humanity says "Thank you" for God's love by sharing it with and showing it to others.

New Year's Day

While New Year's Day is truly a universal holiday, it is not universally celebrated on the same day! The cause of this development is the lack of communication between ancient civilizations, as well as the varied religious and cultural traditions of these societies. For example, the ancient Egyptians celebrated New Year's in the middle of June, when the banks of the Nile River would overflow its banks. Chinese, Jewish, Roman and Islamic calendars also had differing dates for their year's first day, each for different reasons.

In spite of the differences, however, every new year was celebrated with great fanfare and special ceremonies. In many other countries gift-giving constitutes a major part of new year celebrations. This tradition dates back thousands of years, which began when people would bring gifts to different gods or their temples. In ancient Rome, Janus was the god of gates and doors, as well as beginnings and endings. Hence Janus, a god which had two faces, one looking forward, the other backward, received the gifts of the people. Our word *January* originates from this god's name. The motivation of giving gifts to Janus seems to have been, "Perhaps my new year will be better," or "I will receive his blessing this year if I offer a gift." Higher governing officials were also known to have received gifts of all kinds at new year's.

Visiting friends and/or family members has been part of other countries' celebrations. Since people didn't travel too much in older times, the new year gave people an excuse to visit those they otherwise wouldn't see on a regular basis. It gave them an opportunity to catch up on the previous year's events and ask about plans for the future.

In the British Isles, the early English believed that cleaning their chimneys would bring them good luck. Thus, to clean a chimney on New Year's Day would bring blessing to the whole year! This custom was widely practiced for hundreds of years. It also gave birth to the saying, "Cleaning the slate," a reference to this activity. Today when we say this phrase, it means to erase what is already past and begin again or start over.

New Year's Day became an official church holiday in 487AD when it was declared the Feast of the Circumcision. This holiday began without the rowdy parties that were customary of the times. Eventually this custom changed and parties were later permitted. January 1st became widely recognized as New Year's Day in the 1500s with the introduction of the Gregorian calendar.

In the US New Year's Day has **five primary customs**. The **first** is New Year's Eve parties, where people celebrate the hopes and dreams of the coming year. The national symbol of this is the great descending luminous ball in New York City. Each year tens of thousands of well-wishers gather in Times Square to count down the last hours and minutes of the old year. There is much merry making, singing and celebrating. The struggles and difficulties of life in the old year seem to create a sense of optimism in Americans for the coming new year. Whether or not there is any concrete reason for such optimism is not necessary for the American.

The **second** new year custom increasing over the years is the use of fireworks on New Year's Eve. In most states this activity among private citizens requires a special permit. Many people will stay up until midnight and announce the arrival of the new year with a broad display of firecrackers, rockets, flares, etc. This custom is very similar to the Chinese custom of fireworks celebrations at New Year's.

The **third** tradition is the proliferation of football "bowl" games that dominate television. The last week of the year features at least one football game each night in most viewing areas. This custom seems to be related more with the end of the football season than with any particular significance to the coming of a new year. Thus its connection with the arrival of the new year is primarily coincidental. Nevertheless, some make note of this relationship.

The **fourth** custom of New Year's is the New Year's Day parade. Similar to Thanksgiving Day parades, numerous floats, marching bands, huge balloons in the shape of popular characters (especially cartoon figures) are significant parts of these parades. They are held in the mornings and are nationally televised. They seem to capture the excitement and anticipation on the first day of the newly arrived year.

Finally, the **fifth** custom is the making of new year's resolutions. These are commitments an individual makes to change personal behavior. Not all people make resolutions, but many do. Nearly half of all resolutions are broken by the end of January because they usually involve dramatic or major changes in lifestyle that are simply unrealistic or unattainable. Some examples would be: stop smoking, stop drinking, go on a diet, start saving (more) money, read a certain number of books a year, or almost any other personally beneficial behavior change. Resolutions reflect more of an awareness of things that need changing and the desire to change, but do not necessarily include a good plan to actually make those changes. This lack of planning and follow-through explains to a large degree why most resolutions fail before the end of January.

For Christian people, the end of one year and the beginning of another indicates many things. Much like the two-faced Janus, Christians look back at the old year and see another year in which God was faithful and provided for them. They also look forward to the new year by anticipating what God's will for them might be. Some Christians also make new commitments to Him at this time. Many churches will have what is called a "Watch-Night" service on New Year's Eve, which usually consists of things like prayer, fellowship, testimonies, candles, personal and Biblical messages.

Since the Bible teaches that Jesus Christ will return to earth, Christians also anticipate that the new year might be the year of His return to the earth. While this is promised in the Bible, the exact date or time is not given. Thus Christians have a continuing hope of seeing the Lord sooner as time continues. According to the Bible, after Jesus returns He will take His people to Heaven. Things like disasters, pain, suffering, being alone, sickness, and darkness will exist no more for God's people. Obviously their hope is something specific and wonderful. Thus their excitement as New Year's Day approaches.

Martin Luther King Day

Martin Luther King Day is the most recent addition of federally paid national holidays. It is celebrated on January 15th, the birthday of slain civil rights leader, Martin Luther King. In spite of his too short life, King's accomplishments are numerous and impressive.

The second born child of Pastor Michael King, Martin was born in 1929 and raised in Atlanta, Georgia during the Great Depression. He excelled in school and after high school graduation, he attended Morehouse College. In 1948 he graduated from Morehouse with a B.A. in sociology. From there he went to Crozer Theological Seminary and received a B.D. in 1951. Next was Boston University where he received a doctorate of philosophy in 1955.

During his time at Boston University, he met and married Coretta Scott in 1953. A year later he assumed his first pastorate at the Dexter Avenue Baptist Church. He was in Montgomery, Alabama less than a year when Rosa Parks became the focal point of social discrimination against black Americans when she refused to give up her seat to a white man on a full bus. Typically Blacks gave up their seats and stood if Whites were present. With the help of Rev. Ralph Abernathy, King helped organize a one year bus boycott. His effort launched him into national prominence by 1956. In 1958 he wrote his first book, *Stride Toward Freedom*, which not only added to his fame, but elucidated his ideas. Two years later he became the co-pastor with his father of Ebenezer Baptist Church in Atlanta. He also was selected leader of the Southern Christian Leadership Conference (SCLC), a civil rights organization, in 1960.

At the heart of King's motives was a concern for equality for Black Americans. In spite of their technical freedom in the United States, initially granted by Abraham Lincoln, America's 16th President, Blacks continued to be treated as second class citizens under the "separate but equal" understanding of the law. Thus, Whites and Blacks might eat at the same restaurant, but in separate rooms. More often, they weren't allowed to eat in the same place, or do a host of other things together. If they rode the bus, for example, Blacks sat in the back, Whites in the front. Even simple things like restrooms and water fountains were segregated. It was like this throughout the south, with little hope of things changing. His impassioned "I Have A Dream" speech in 1964 on the steps of the Lincoln Memorial in Washington, DC, was undoubtedly his finest hour. *Time* magazine named him "Man of the Year." Later that same year he received the Nobel Peace Prize, the first black American to do so. At age 35, he was also the youngest person ever to win this award.

By 1965, however, a shift began as the result of King's observations that social discrimination was contributing to economic discrimination. He began calling for a "revolution of values," and changes in governmental policies toward Blacks. This attracted others to join in the numerous marches, boycotts, rallies and strikes. Some people began questioning a number of his associates, but he persevered in spite of the criticism. By 1968 he was in Washington, DC demanding a $12 billion "Economic Bill of Rights," insisting that until social discrimination was a thing of the past, economic relief for Black Americans was required. Some Americans withdrew their support of him, not appreciating this focus on financial relief from the government. They believed it went too far.

In the middle of this Washington crusade, King went to Memphis, Tennessee to help support a strike by sanitation workers in April, 1968. While standing out on the rear balcony of the motel operating as his headquarters on April 4th, King was shot by a lone gunman, James Earl Ray. King died that night, at the age of 39. The civil rights leader of millions, who read and followed the teachings of Jesus and Gandhi's non-violent civil disobedience, became the victim of a violent death. Throughout the next months, many cities all across the US suffered from riots, looting, civil strife, death and property damage caused by many who were angry over King's death and the way he died. Police, army reserves, and the National Guard finally restored order, but not without great difficulty, injuries and loss of life. Ray was convicted of the crime and imprisoned.

More than any other man in America, Martin Luther King raised Americans' awareness of the struggles of a minority group within her borders. As the one who began to point to the differences in people, and the acceptance of those differences, history understands him to be one of the earliest proponents of the modern concept of diversity, a man ahead of his time. In 1983 the Congress of the United States passed a law declaring King's birthday, January 15th, a national holiday. Because some Americans saw him not so much as a great American leader but a controversial one, it took years before all the states fully complied with the law. Celebrations will include rallies, demonstrations, speeches, marches and media presentations on the civil rights movement and on King's life. Regardless of perceptions, his impact on American society is still being felt today.

The values of non-discrimination and acceptance that he championed are clearly taught in the Bible. The Scripture states that God does not discriminate on the basis of outward appearance (see 1 Samuel 16:7) and neither should his people (James 2:1-13). Martin Luther King's legacy is a reminder that the dignity of all people, regardless of race, language, ethnicity, cultural or national background, ought to be uppermost in our minds.

Presidents' Day

Presidents' Day came about by combining the birthdays of two American presidents: George Washington and Abraham Lincoln. Its origins began by Americans who celebrated Washington's birthday, February 22nd. Lincoln's birthday is February 12th and because of his legacy, some felt his birthday should also be recognized. A compromise was reached when a floating holiday, known as Presidents' Day, would be celebrated on the third Monday in February. The date of this holiday always falls in between the two presidents' birthdays.

Washington is known as "the father of his country" and is one of those "larger than life" historical figures who is known around the world. He was born in 1732 in Pope's Creek, VA, the oldest son of Augustine and Mary Washington. When George was 11 his father died, and he considered joining the British navy. His mother would not allow this, so he took up surveying. In 1753 he got involved in the French and Indian War as a scout. Gaining name recognition from his military adventures, he entered politics in 1759 and was selected to Virginia's House of Burgesses. Earlier that year he married Martha Custis, a wealthy widow who had two children, John and "Patsy." They had no children of their own.

Tensions between the American colonies and Great Britain grew, and by 1769 Washington was leading Virginia's opposition to England's colonial policies. After two meetings of the Continental Congress (1774-75), the Congress unanimously chose him to be Commander-in-Chief of the Continental Army, which he assumed July 3, 1775. After some major losses, serious deprivations, providential escapes and dramatic victories, Washington's army surrounded and captured General Cornwallis' forces at Yorktown, VA on September 28, 1781. The defeat of the British army gave Americans their independence. During the war, Washington's stature and reputation grew immense, largely due to the stories many loyal soldiers would tell of his concern, integrity and faith in God. Some saw him alone on his knees in the woods, praying for his soldiers, the war effort and divine guidance.

After the war Washington was eager to retire from public life and returned to his beloved home, Mount Vernon, a large estate of five farms. He grew wheat and fruit trees, among other crops, and was an expert farmer, using crop rotation to prevent mineral depletion in the soil. But his peers had other ideas for their general. In 1787 he was chosen to lead Virginia's delegation to the Constitutional Convention. Once the Constitution was written, Washington was unanimously elected the first President of the United States and inaugurated on April 30, 1789. After a rather uneventful first term where many precedents were set, he was elected again to another 4 year term in 1792. He dealt with more difficult matters his second term, which added to what was formerly very muted and limited public criticism. He briefly considered a third term, but decided against it. His Farewell Address, given in 1797, became a benchmark for American foreign policy for well over a hundred years. After less than three years' retirement, Washington succumbed to a brief illness. He died December 14, 1799.

Washington was universally lauded for his character, his moral understanding, his faith in Christ, and his care for his fellow man. He was described as being "First in war, first in peace, and first in the hearts of his countrymen." Funeral services and mourning continued for months after his death. His birthday was immediately identified as a national holiday. Washington, DC and the Washington Monument are named for him. His figure appears on the one dollar bill and 25 cent quarter.

On the other hand Abraham Lincoln, known as "Honest Abe," came from a rather unassuming background and was an unlikely character for greatness. Born in 1809 in Hardin (now Larue) County, KY within a decade of Washington's death, Abraham was named for a grandfather who was killed by Native Americans. His father, Thomas, had no formal education but was a skilled carpenter. Because of his family's Baptist background, they opposed slavery and soon moved to Indiana, a "free" state. The death of his mother Nancy when Abraham was only 9 left a deep scar on him. The next year his father married Sarah Bush Johnston whom Abraham respected and admired, and she continued his religious and moral instruction from the Bible. Abraham would read anything he could get his hands on, and frequently read by candlelight in his family's dark log cabin. He had particular respect for many of the country's founders, especially Washington.

In 1828 he took his first trip, traveling down the Mississippi River to New Orleans. Two years later he moved to Illinois, and in 1831 settled near Springfield. The next year he ran unsuccessfully for the Illinois legislature. He won the next election in 1834 and served in the legislature until 1841. During that time he became a lawyer and also married Mary Todd, a Presbyterian, on November 4, 1842. They had four sons.

In 1847 his political ambitions turned national in scope, and he served one term in the US House of Representatives as a member of the Whig Party. In 1856 he changed to the newly formed Republican Party which had a clearly defined platform against slavery on moral grounds. He ran against Stephen Douglas for the Senate in 1858. Seven debates were held between the two men during the campaign, and Lincoln's principles, morals, logic and vocabulary put him in favorable national standing. Lincoln won the debates but lost the election to Douglas.

Based on their understanding of his personal qualities, moral arguments and national esteem, the Republican Party selected Lincoln to run for President in 1860. He won a plurality of votes among several other candidates, including northern and southern Democrats, which split the vote among that party. He became the nation's sixteenth president. The South considered Lincoln's victory and the Republican "anti-slavery" platform to be the end of any hopes of reconciliation with the North. By the time he was inaugurated in March, 1861, the Southern states had seceded from the Union. Within five weeks of his presidency, the Civil War began and brought on the darkest days of American history and the most deadly conflict ever to hit the United States.

While regionalized thinking within the US had been building for years, the hostilities formally began in Charleston harbor of South Carolina on April 12, 1861 when Confederate artillery fired upon the Union's Fort Sumter. Eighteen months later, on September 24, 1862 Lincoln showed moral courage when, under current war conditions, he issued his "Emancipation Proclamation" which technically freed the slaves. He felt the Constitution protected the right to slavery during peacetime. But the war continued and was fought in several areas around the country. Gettysburg, PA was the location of one particularly costly battle, and Lincoln addressed the dedication of a cemetery there with his "Gettysburg Address," a concise but brilliant speech which not only addressed the slaughter of the war, but also outlined his thinking for the future of the country. It is considered a classic among great political speeches.

Lincoln went through a number of generals before settling on Ulysses S. Grant in 1864. The South had much better military leadership but lacked the industrialized strength and supply capabilities of the North. Later victories by the North helped Lincoln win re-election. Later that year with the end of the war in sight, he looked forward to restoring a wounded country. Five days after the Southern Commanding General Robert E. Lee surrendered, on April 14th Lincoln with his wife went to Ford's Theater in Washington, DC to watch a performance of *Our American Cousin* as a distraction from the worries of war. At the theater, a nationally renowned actor and slavery sympathizer, John Wilkes Booth, slipped past a drunk military guard, ascended the stairs to the Presidential booth and shot Lincoln in the back of the head. It was Good Friday, the weekend of the Easter celebration. He was carried unconscious to the building across the street where he died the next morning at 7:22AM. Booth was later caught and killed for his crime.

Lincoln's hope of seeing the restoration of the country he loved was cut short. A funeral train traveled back across the US with the body of "Father Abraham," as he was affectionately known by his admirers. He was buried in Springfield, IL on May 4th. The war already concluded, Lincoln in many respects had become its last victim. Even with some personal flaws and bouts of depression, and having been criticized for some of his policies, historians have long agreed that Lincoln was a unique man for a unique time. More than anything else his sheer determination and strength of character kept the United States together. His gentle spirit was reflected in his second inaugural address in which he called for "malice toward none," and "charity for all." To that end he gave his life. His figure appears on the 5 dollar bill and the one cent penny. The Lincoln Memorial is his tribute in the nation's capital.

President's Day is set aside as a national holiday which honors Washington and Lincoln. Both of them were known for their strong moral character and their faith in the truths of the Bible. The circumstances and opportunities of history only served to magnify their integrity and complete dependence on God. It was these and related qualities that helped forge the national character of the United States. It is also why these men are universally regarded as the two greatest American presidents. Most celebrations of Presidents' Day will have historic or patriotic overtones. Raised American flags, parades and speeches will be accompanied with picnics and other activities.

Valentine's Day

Valentine's Day is a one-day celebration of romance and love held on February 14th. Like many American holidays, it has a combination of ancient Greek and Roman elements and more recent church connections. We'll examine them in their historical order.

The Romans had many gods in their pantheon and related celebrations. The festival of *Lupercalia* was celebrated on February 15th in honor of a god and goddess. The first was Faunus, a rural Italian god who later became associated with Pan, the god of nature, herds and fertility. Sacrifices and ceremonies were held at Lupercal, a cave in the Palatine Hill, also the home of Juno, the goddess of women and marriage. Celebrations would include women randomly choosing a partner to show signs of affection and gifts. These relationships endured long after the festival was over, and many ended in marriage. Thus Cupid, the Roman god of love, known as Eros to the Greeks, later became associated with *Lupercalia*.

The first images of Cupid show him to be a strong, handsome young man with wings. By the mid-300's BC, his image had changed to that of a chubby male baby with wings who carried a bow and arrows. As the story is told, those whom Cupid shot with an arrow would fall in love. Cupid remains a central figure in current day Valentine's Day images.

As with many of the Western holidays, when Christianity spread through Europe, the Roman Catholic Church attempted to give Christian meaning to the holiday. In 496 AD, Pope Gelasius changed the *Lupercalia* festival by moving it one day earlier to February 14th and called it Saint Valentine's Day. The background of St. Valentine is not at all clear. One or possibly two historical figures could be the infamous St. Valentine. One possible candidate was a priest who lived in Rome under the rule of Emperor Claudius II in the 200's AD. His "crime" was helping persecuted Christians, and the Romans jailed him. Sometime around 270 AD he was beheaded on Palatine Hill, the site of Juno's alter. Valentine was therefore a natural choice to replace the *Lupercalia* festivities with a more Christian idea of love. Valentine's remains are buried in the St. Praxedes Church in Rome. Another Valentine supposedly lived around the same time and was beheaded for converting a Roman family to Christianity. It is possible that the two Valentines are one and the same person. In both cases, Valentine was a man who was true to his faith and loved those around him, even to the point of death.

In spite of the attempts of the Church, much of the sentimentality of the original holiday remained. European countries have various Valentine traditions and customs. The earliest customs can be traced to as far back as the 1400's, when Geoffrey Chaucer, the most famous English poet of the Middle Ages (author of *Canterbury Tales*), mentioned that he noticed birds would pair off first on February 14th. Many of the customs still involved a random pairing off of girls and boys who would become each other's Valentine. Typically gifts or Valentine tokens were exchanged. Activities also included rather superstitious activities where a single female could "catch" a man that she might later marry. In England in the 1700's, expressions of sentimentality between Valentines began to replace gift giving as the main feature of the holiday.

Valentine celebrations in America didn't begin until the 1800's. By 1863 a magazine article stated that besides Christmas, Valentine's Day had become the most celebrated holiday in the world! Modern-day school children will celebrate Valentine's Day by making handmade cards for friends and family members. Such cards usually are red and white, include heart shaped cut-outs, lace paper and doilies, and contain messages of fondness and affection. Pictures of Cupid will appear on many professionally made cards in card stores. These cards will contain messages of love, commitment, passion, or sometimes be humorous and amusing. Adults will celebrate the day with gestures of love and commitment to their Valentine (presumably their spouse, girlfriend or boyfriend). Things like flowers, candy, a romantic night out, a favorite meal, a special gift or almost anything else can be appropriate. Many couples even planned their wedding around Valentine's Day, making it their anniversary.

Today Valentine's Day is a day to reaffirm one's love for another. Some Christians take advantage of this day by remembering the great love that God has for the world. Just as the original Valentine died helping those around him, God sent his son Jesus who likewise gave his life for those who wanted to establish a relationship with him. One famous verse in the Bible, John 3:16 says, *For God so loved the world that he gave his one and only son, that whoever believes in him shall not perish but have eternal life*. Thus Valentine's Day can serve as a useful reminder of the greatest love known to man: God's love. It gives Christians an opportunity to share it with their neighbors, friends and loved ones, just like the original Valentine.

St. Patrick's Day

Saint Patrick's Day is March 17th of each year. It is a day of remembrance and honor for the second bishop (after Palladius) of Ireland, Saint Patrick. March 17th is the day the Roman Catholic Church chose for the festive celebration. A brief biography of Patrick follows.

Patrick was born in 389AD to a Christian Anglo-Saxon family in southwestern Britain which was under Roman rule at the time. Although he had a Christian upbringing, he had little to do with Christianity. When he was only 16 years old, he was captured by Irish raiding pirates and taken back to Ireland and enslaved, herding pigs. While he was there he saw many cruelties committed by the non-Christian Irish. This brought him to the realization that he needed God's forgiveness for his own sins. His time there also gave him the vision that the Irish needed Christianity. Then, while praying one night after 6 years in captivity, Patrick believed God gave him an escape plan. Following the plan precisely, he took a ship to Gaul (present day France) and later returned to his family in Britain.

For the next 20 years (412 - 431AD) Patrick, motivated to bring Christianity to Ireland, returned to Gaul and spent his time studying the Bible with Germanus at Auxerre. (Germanus was Bishop of Auxerre and led two successful expeditions to Britain; his feast day is July 31st.) He returned to his family in Britain where God impressed him in a dream to return to the Irish. Resisting the pleas of his family, Patrick again went to Auxerre and received the appointment and blessing from Germanus as the Bishop of the Irish in 432AD.

Patrick began his work in northern and western Ireland. He had mixed results when he first arrived. He intended to visit his former slave owner, Miliucc, and share the message of Christ with him. But

Miliucc, hearing Patrick was coming and fearing his revenge, killed himself before he arrived. Patrick had some early successes among the poor, but he soon realized that if he were to be truly successful, he would need to gain the favor of the rulers. Irish society at that time was dominated by the Druids. So the Bishop publicly confronted them at Tara, the royal center of Ireland. Gradually he was able to convince numerous tribal leaders to accept Christianity, including King Loegaire (pronounced LEER ee). This resulted in obvious momentum for his ministry.

By the end of his ministry, Patrick had developed 450 church leaders who helped start over 300 churches resulting in over 120,000 baptisms. He saw the whole country change its legal code and base it on Biblical principles. In spite of these great accomplishments, however, the new Irish converts resisted the Catholic system of church structure, something for which Patrick was criticized by British clergymen. Patrick died in 461AD.

Legend has it that in his sermons Patrick would use a 3-leaf clover called a "shamrock" to represent the Trinity (the Triune God). Thus a 4-leaf clover, a rare item in nature, was said to represent God's special blessing. Over the years this idea came to mean "good luck," and became synonymous with being "lucky." A common expression that developed was called "the luck of the Irish," and some people today still consider the Irish to be lucky.

St. Patrick's Day is a festive occasion for many, but especially for Catholics who made him a patron saint. On March 17 people traditionally wear something green (the color of choice, no doubt coming from green clovers). Later, a childish prank was added: If you didn't wear something green on that day, you could be pinched! Modern celebrations will include parades, church services, picnics and parties. As with many holiday celebrations in America, it seems that many, if not most, Americans are largely unaware of the historic events leading to the modern celebration of St. Patrick's Day.

Easter

Easter is the common name given to the annual Christian celebration of the resurrection of Jesus Christ. The date of Easter each year is the first Sunday after the first full moon on or after March 21st. Thus Easter always occurs between March 22nd and April 25th. The first Nicene Council in 325AD decided to use a lunar basis for setting the date. American Easter practices and customs have a mixture of both Biblical and pagan elements. We will first consider the historical events surrounding the resurrection and then examine how the pagan factors were later added.

Jesus of Nazareth lived for about 33 years (4BC - 30AD) in Israel. The Bible indicates that He was called "the Christ," meaning *The Chosen One* or *The Anointed One.* This surname identified Him as the long awaited "Messiah," the Hebrew equivalent. Hundreds of predictions in early portions of the Bible (the Old Testament) made reference to the life of this special servant of God. He was to be God's unique representative on earth. He would be the leader of God's people. And He would be personally responsible for taking the consequence of mankind's evil and disobedience on Himself. Since God's punishment for evil and disobedience was death, Jesus willingly chose to die as a substitutionary sacrifice for others. Because He was God in human form, He kept God's Law perfectly, and thus was the only one able to meet God's requirement.

According to tradition Jesus died on a Friday. He was executed by being nailed through His hands and feet to a cross of wood, the common form of death for criminals in the Roman Empire. Death was usually prolonged and tortuous, but Jesus died after only six hours, due to His weakened condition from the severe beating and whipping He received previously. The Bible says that His death is sufficient payment for mankind's evil. Initially Christians celebrated the Crucifixion and Resurrection as one event, but in the fourth century the Crucifixion developed its own focus and gradually became known as "Good Friday." It was good because God kept His promise by removing the penalty for evil and disobedience through Christ and His death.

Jesus was buried in an above-ground grave called *a tomb*. The Bible indicates that on the third day He rose physically and literally from the dead early Sunday morning, before the sun came up. Over the next several weeks He showed himself to His followers. The Scripture reveals that His body showed the same physical features, including the wounds He received at His death. He also had physical capacities, demonstrated when He ate in their presence. But His was also a "spiritual" body — one that would die no more. Jesus also said that because of what had happened to Him, people all over the world could now be forgiven, establish a relationship with God through Christ, and know that they would see God and be with Him when they died. This message of forgiveness to anyone who would believe or put their confidence in Christ was good news, and remains good news for people today. It is what gives Christians their motivation to spread the message of Christ. Thus Easter, increasingly called *Resurrection Day* by Christians, is their most important holy day. (Forty days after His resurrection Jesus ascended from the earth and returned to Heaven.) The details of these accounts can be found in the Biblical books of Matthew (chapters 26-28), Mark (14-16), Luke (22-24) and John (18-21).

As noted earlier, pagan elements began to be associated with the resurrection celebration. The very name "Easter" appears to have come from the Teutonic (ancient Germanic) goddess of spring, *Eostre*. The spring festival was called *Eostur*. It is more than obvious how the name was transferred.

However, long before this, the use of eggs became a popular custom. From very ancient times eggs have represented the new life that returns during the spring. Ancient Persians and Egyptians dyed their eggs in spring colors and gave them to friends as gifts. Christians in Mesopotamia first adopted this custom of using and coloring eggs as part of the Christian celebration.

In various countries where Easter has long been celebrated, egg decorations will be slightly different. In the US eggs are also made of chocolate and candy. Hollow plastic eggs are filled with treats and kept in Easter baskets. The baskets are used in Easter egg hunts, an activity for children. Eggs are hidden in a yard or rooms of a house. Then children are given baskets and told to find as many eggs as possible. The one who finds the most eggs usually wins a prize.

The "Easter Bunny" also has long been connected with this celebration. However, the bunny, like the egg tradition, has more of a pagan connection to the season of spring than to the Resurrection. In ancient Egypt the rabbit symbolizes birth and new life. Egyptians also connected the rabbit with the moon. Because Easter is determined by the lunar calendar, the rabbit or bunny became an Easter symbol. Many children in the US think that it is the Easter bunny that brings and hides the Easter eggs. In 1878 President Rutherford B. Hayes began the tradition of inviting children to the White House for an Easter egg-rolling contest. This custom continues to this day.

Many church calendars are based on and developed around Easter. *Lent* is the 40 day preparation period immediately before Easter. This period is marked by prayer, fasting or other personal sacrifices. The first day of Lent is called "Ash Wednesday." The day before that is called "Shrove Tuesday." The Sunday before Easter is "Palm Sunday," so named because when Jesus went to Jerusalem in triumph the Sunday before He died, His followers created a pathway made of cut palm branches. The Thursday before Easter is called "Maundy Thursday" which is followed by Good Friday. Many churches will have special services on these days.

On Easter Sunday, many Christians attend a sunrise service, sometimes calling it a "Son-Rise" service, named for Jesus being the Son of God who rose from the dead. Other celebrations would include parades, plays and dramas, concerts and cantatas. During this time of year movies centered around the life of Jesus can be seen on television. Some well-known titles are *Jesus, Jesus of Nazareth, The Robe, Ben-Hur* and *The Greatest Story Ever Told*. Most, if not all, of these films can be rented in video form in many video outlets.

The uniqueness of the Christian message depends on Jesus' resurrection. His body is not in the tomb. "He has risen!" Christians say, as does the Bible. If it could be proven that Jesus were still dead and buried, Christians would have no hope or anything in which to believe.

One Christian writer, Paul, writes a thorough and logical presentation about the necessity and centrality of the resurrection in 1 Corinthians chapter 15 in the Bible. In this chapter he states clearly that the reality of Christ's resurrection guarantees the resurrection of all others to face God.

Skeptics have offered numerous theories to explain away the disappearance of Christ's body. All such theories break down due to the available evidence and testimony that counter their claims. As long as opponents of Christianity cannot produce a credible explanation of the disappearance of Christ's body, Christians will have strong, historical testimony to support their belief and strengthen their confidence in Biblical teaching. Thus Easter is an annual reminder of all they believe and cherish.

Memorial Day

Memorial Day is a truly patriotic holiday which falls on May 30th, but is celebrated on the last Monday in May. It is a day set aside for remembering and honoring those who died while serving in the American Armed Forces. It includes all deceased military service personnel. This holiday has also been called "Decoration Day," and is the unofficial beginning of summer.

This holiday had a rather informal beginning, around the time of the American Civil War (1861-1865). More Americans died in this war (about 500,000) than in any other US war. According to tradition, some women of the Confederate States of America (CSA, the southern states that seceded from the Union), chose May 30th to decorate the graves of Civil War soldiers. They decorated the graves of both Union and Confederate soldiers. Then in 1868 General John A. Logan proclaimed May 30th as a special day for honoring those Union soldiers who died in the war. Logan was Commander-in-chief of the Grand Army of the Republic, an organization of the Union's Civil War veterans. They adopted the term "Memorial Day" as the official name. Annual celebrations were held in many of the northern states. Responsibilities for Memorial Day activities later passed to the American Legion. The Legion was founded in Paris in 1919. It is the largest American veterans organization, having over 3 million members who meet at over 16,000 posts or assembly halls. Its primary purpose is the well-being of veterans.

After World War I veterans groups began selling small, red artificial flowers called "poppies" as a token memorial for people to wear as part of remembering those who died in battle. The idea came from Europe. After the war many of the battlefields in France bloomed with bright poppies, showing the renewal of life there. As a result the week leading up to Memorial Day was called "Poppy Week" in some parts of the country. Graves of war dead were also decorated with poppies. Proceeds from poppy sales helped disabled and needy veterans' causes. This practice is not quite as popular today, since most of the World War veterans have died. Veterans organizations raise funds through other methods.

In 1971 Congress passed a law making Memorial Day a national holiday. It is held on the last Monday of May all across the US. Originally it honored those who died in the Civil War, Spanish-American War (1898), World Wars I and II (1917-18 and 1941-45 respectively), the Korean War (1950-53). It now includes those who gave their lives in the Vietnam War (1961-74) and the more recent Persian Gulf War (1991).

Typical Memorial Day celebrations include parades (often including Boy Scouts, Girl Scouts, fraternal and other groups), special programs that include speeches, the reading of Abraham Lincoln's "Gettysburg Address" (a brief speech commemorating those who died at the battle of Gettysburg, PA in the Civil War), prayers and moments of silence, and military exercises and demonstrations. Port cities with military installations often will host ceremonies for sailors and navy personnel who died at sea. These services are similar to those mentioned earlier, but will include tiny ships containing flowers or wreaths made of flowers. These are set afloat as a memorial. Americans will also attend picnics and baseball games, go sightseeing or boating, take trips, barbecue outdoors, and almost any other kind of open social event made possible by the freedom these soldiers died to protect.

People of the Christian faith see a spiritual application to Memorial Day. According to Biblical writings and history, Jesus died in a spiritual struggle for the destiny of mankind. Without His death, which paid for man's sins, all humanity was lost, and had no future with God. Because of Christ's sacrifice, Christians enjoy a relationship with God and know their sins are forgiven. Therefore many churches have special services with a Memorial Day theme. Similarly churches also have a traditional memorial of Jesus' death. It is called a variety of names, including *Communion Service, The Lord's Supper, The Lord's Table, The Eucharist,* and others. Churches vary on how often this service is held. Some celebrate it every week, while others have it one, four, six or twelve times a year.

Independence Day

Independence Day, also known as the Fourth of July, is not only a truly significant national holiday, but also one for other parts of the world. It was on July 4, 1776 that the thirteen struggling American Colonies collectively decided to declare their independence from the most powerful country on earth. To the surprise of many, the United States of America not only succeeded, but also thrived as no other country in the world in the last 200+ years. Those who boldly stated their freedom from England in the *Declaration of Independence* were among the same leaders who wrote the *United States Constitution* which forged a government that has stood longer than any other in the world. Because of the survivability of our government, many other nations have respected it and attempted to copy our success. Events leading to the signing of the *Declaration* and Independence Day follow.

As the American colonial population grew in numbers, it slowly became obvious to many that developments in North America were significantly different than those in other British colonies. The First Great Awakening of the mid 1700's, a revival of fervent Christianity, had aroused the religious interest and passion of tens of thousands of Americans. In contrast, no such enthusiasm had come to Britain. Americans increasingly felt an allegiance first to God and then to England. The English didn't seem to appreciate such sentiments, especially when Americans disagreed with their English rulers.

At this time in history "revolutionary" ideas were increasingly common. They began originally with England's *Magna Carta*, meaning "great charter." It was the first historical step towards a constitutional government. This document, written in June of 1215, contained 63 articles and stated the rights of various classes of individuals. It also paved the way for elected, representative government. In England this is called Parliament. In the 1600's the *Magna Carta* was being used to expand the constitutional check on despotic kings and rulers. It helped in England's own "Glorious Revolution" which brought William and Mary to the throne in the bloodless revolt of 1688. Philosopher John Locke advanced the ideas of contractual government and natural rights under God. Sir William Blackstone, a famous British lawyer, cited the *Magna Carta* as a basis for the rights of common people under a constitutional government in the 1700's. Many of these ideas found their way to the American colonies. Indeed, the *Mayflower Compact* of 1620 had already set a precedent of liberty under God as a governmental form on the American continent.

As a result, by the middle 1700's the Colonies appealed to Britain for a greater share in colonial policy decisions. Greatest among the issues was taxation. In 1765 Parliament passed the Stamp Act which required a tax on all official papers and documents, including newspapers and other various items. The American protest, captured in the slogan, "No taxation without representation," was so strong that the act was repealed a year later. Not to be outdone by the complaints, Parliament then passed a law giving it the sole responsibility for legislating the Colonies. More taxes created more protests; protests brought tax removals, but the tax on tea, the symbol of English lifestyle, remained. The refusal to remove this particular tax resulted in the "Boston Tea Party" in 1773 when colonists disguised as Native Americans secretly boarded British ships in Boston harbor and dumped large cargoes of tea into the water. This action was copied by other colonists in other harbors later.

Parliament's response was predictable. They imposed a whole series of mandates which Americans called the Intolerable Acts. These were designed to make life miserable for the colonists. In 1774 the Colonies knew that they needed to stand united if they were to survive. With the exception of Georgia, they elected delegates and sent them to Philadelphia, PA, for the First Continental Congress. They met during September and October and decided for which rights they needed to stand. They chose to discontinue trade with England and not use British goods. They also agreed to meet in one year if Parliament had not changed their policies by then.

English disposition remained resolute — they were not about to change. In fact, they felt more needed to be done to disarm the Colonies from engaging in more serious hostilities. The British ordered General Thomas Gage to destroy the Colonists' main supply depot at Concord, MA. 700 British soldiers, known as "Redcoats," arrived in Lexington on the way to Concord on April 19, 1775. A small band of American patriots, warned by Paul Revere on his famous ride, showed up with muskets and rifles. After a skirmish which lasted less than 15 minutes, 8 patriots lay dead with 10 wounded. One Redcoat was wounded. This was the famous battle that fired "the shot heard 'round the world," according to Ralph Waldo Emerson. By the time the British reached Concord, the supplies had been hidden, and another battle followed. However, the patriots had increased their numbers and after several volleys the Redcoats retreated. The Colonists shot at the British discriminately from behind trees and bushes, and by the end of the day, 250 redcoats had been killed, while American losses were under 100. In June, the Battle of Bunker Hill was successfully fought and one month later George Washington accepted the leadership of the Continental Army. Other battles later that year broke out in Montreal and Quebec, Canada. In December, the British Parliament voted to declare war on the American Colonies.

The British declaration of war only intensified Colonial feelings for independence. Samuel Adams asked what many were thinking, "Is not America already independent? Why not then declare it?" British writer Thomas Paine's pamphlet *Common Sense* also excited the patriots with his lucid arguments for American freedom. Patrick Henry gave a memorable speech in Virginia where he said, "Give me liberty or give me death!" Town meetings in Massachusetts and people in Virginia approved of independence. Thus the discussions of the Second Continental Congress, which assembled on May 10, 1775 in the Old State House (now called Independence Hall) in Philadelphia, began focusing on the war effort and independence. On June 7 Virginia delegate Richard Henry Lee introduced a resolution to Congress, "That these United Colonies are, and of a right ought to be, free and independent States..." Three days later Congress named a committee to write such a declaration. Five men were chosen for this committee: John Adams, Benjamin Franklin, Thomas Jefferson, Robert Livingstone and Roger Sherman. Jefferson was asked to do the writing because of his recognized skill. Congress then adjourned for 3 weeks so that representatives could better understand the will of their constituents.

After reassembling, Lee's resolution was approved on July 2nd. Debate then began over Jefferson's draft, which had taken him about 2 weeks to write. He borrowed from the many church sermons of the day as well as from current political phraseology. He modified the trinity of inalienable rights of "life, liberty and property" to "life, liberty and the pursuit of happiness" (the change of the last item meaning *civic duty*). Delegates entered into what John Adams called, "the greatest debate of all," and reviewed the whole text. With the exception of two phrases which Congress insisted on including, they agreed to its contents. John Hancock was the first to sign the document. Thus the *Declaration of Independence* was approved on July 4, 1776, after serious deliberation and a lot of prayer. After the vote some men wept. Others stared out the window. Some bowed their heads. Samuel Adams, delegate from Massachusetts, stood up and said, "We have this day restored the Sovereign, to Whom alone men ought to be obedient. He reigns in heaven and...from the rising to the setting sun, may His Kingdom come."

Contrary to many modern perspectives and opinions, at least 50 of the 56 men who approved and signed the *Declaration* were strong, active Christians who believed the Bible and attended church regularly. Their own writings, as well as their conduct, attest to this fact. They saw their resistance to tyranny as obedience to God's commands. They simply wanted to restore government to its rightful place under God's authority. The statement, "We hold these truths to be self-evident, that all men are created equal, that they are endowed by their Creator with certain unalienable rights..." is based on a thoroughly Christian understanding of political philosophy and worldview. It was the first time such words were penned as the basis of a government. While it is still debated today as to whether the United States is or ever was a Christian nation, one thing is clear: from the very beginning the thinking that led to the establishment of the United States was grounded on Biblical principles. Many today cite the longevity of America's government as additional proof of this claim.

Today Christians and non-Christians alike have a special heritage from their country's founders. The ideas of the equality of man, right to life, representative government, freedoms of expression, worship, speech, etc., are dependent on self-control, civic duty, personal responsibility and care for one's neighbor. The founders also largely believed in the inherent evil of man, the necessity of salvation, submission to God and moral responsibility. These are all ideas found in the Bible. Speaking of the *Constitution*, the corollary document to the *Declaration*, signer John Adams would later write, "Our *Constitution* was designed only for a moral and religious people. It is wholly inadequate for the government of any other." Therefore many Christians make a connection between patriotism, civic duty and spiritual service.

After the vote to approve the *Declaration*, Adams, who went on to become America's second president, wrote his wife Abigail saying that the Fourth of July

> *...will be the most memorable...in the history of America. I am apt to believe that it will be celebrated by succeeding generations, as the great anniversary festival. It ought to be commemorated, as the Day of Deliverance, by solemn acts of devotion to God Almighty. It ought to be solemnized with pomp and parade, with shows, games, sports, guns, bells, bonfires and illuminations, from one end of the continent to the other, from this time forward forevermore.*

And so it has been. Normal celebrations will include parades, picnics, patriotic speeches, church services, concerts, and lots of fireworks. Because of the numerous injuries and deaths of citizens during this celebration, the States began in the early 1900's to outlaw the use of fireworks used and handled by private citizens. In spite of this, many citizens still celebrate the holiday with fireworks, guns, and other forms of noisy jubilation.

Churches often will recognize the day with sermons and messages making the obvious connection between civil liberty and spiritual freedom, the latter being found in Christ. The balance between independence and dependence on God is another theme Christians consider important during this holiday, along with civic duty, self-control, moral values of the nation, etc. Today there is a battle currently being fought for the conscience of America, including whose values should be the basis for American society. History clearly records that it was Christian values that established the country. That being true, it should be recognized that Christian values can best maintain and direct the future of America.